A vision from THE HOLY SPIRIT:

A river flowing!
Roaring!
A sunny day!
Inner tubes floating down.
Everyone has their own.
The more fun you have…the more people join in!
The more relaxed you are…the faster you go.
The more you splash and kick, the more you spin around
…for no reason!
and the more difficult it is to stay with the others!
The more drinks, suntan lotion, umbrellas, and other fun stuff you have,
the more people notice.
The more you stay together, the more people notice…and want to join in!
The more you talk and praise with each other the more people notice!

FLOW IN MY RIVER!
YOU ARE IN MY RIVER!
ENJOY MY LOVE!
ENJOY ME!
ENJOY MY LIFE!
…MY
LIFE!

THE RIVER

OF

GOD!

John in his book relays to us how Jesus described THIS RIVER, HIS RIVER:

Jesus therefore, being wearied from His journey sat thus by the well. It was about the sixth hour. A woman of Samaria came down to draw water. Jesus said to her, "Give me a drink". For His disciples had gone away into the city to buy food. Then the woman of Samaria said to Him, "How is that you being a Jew, ask a drink from me, a Samaritan woman?". For Jews have no dealings with Samaritans. Jesus answered and said to her, "If you knew the gift of God, and who it is who says to you, "Give me a drink", you would have asked Him, and He would have given you living water". The woman said to Him, "Sir You have nothing to draw with, and the well is deep. Where then do you get that living water? Are you greater than our father Jacob, who gave us the well, and drank from it himself, as well as his sons and his livestock?"

Jesus answered and said to her, "WHOEVER DRINKS OF THIS WATER WILL THIRST AGAIN. BUT WHOEVER DRINKS OF THE WATER THAT I SHALL GIVE HIM WILL NEVER THIRST. BUT THE WATER THAT I SHALL GIVE HIM WILL BECOME IN HIM A FOUNTAIN OF WATER SPRINGING UP INTO EVERLASTING LIFE".

Ezekiel in the Old Testament also describes to us what God showed him about this RIVER:

Then he brought me back to the door of the temple: and there was water flowing from under the threshold of the temple toward the east, for the front of the temple faced east; the water was flowing from under the right side of the temple, south of the altar. He brought me out by way of the north gate, and led me around on the outside to the outer gateway that faces east; and there was water, running out the right side. And when the man went out to the east with the line in his hand, he measured a thousand cubits, and he brought me through the waters; the water came up to my ankles. Again he measured one thousand and brought me through the waters; the water came up to my knees. Again he measured one thousand and brought me through; the water came up to my waist. Again he measured one thousand, and it was a river that I could not cross; for the water was too deep, water in which no one could swim, a river that could not be crossed.

HE SAID TO ME, "SON OF MAN, HAVE YOU SEEN THIS?" THEN HE BROUGHT ME AND RETURNED ME TO THE BANK OF THE RIVER. WHEN I RETURNED, THERE, ALONG THE BANK OF THE RIVER, WERE VERY MANY TREES ON ONE SIDE AND THE THE OTHER. THEN HE SAID TO ME: "THIS WATER FLOWS TOWARD

THE EAST REGION, GOES DOWN INTO THE VALLEY, AND ENTERS THE SEA. WHEN IT REACHES THE SEA, ITS WATERS ARE HEALED. AND IT SHOULD BE THAT EVERY LIVING THING THAT MOVES, WHEREVER THE RIVERS GO, WILL LIVE. THERE WILL BE GREAT MULTITUDES OF FISH, BECAUSE THESE WATERS GO THERE; FOR THEY WILL BE HEALED, AND EVERYTHING WILL LIVE WHEREVER THE RIVER GOES."

A RIVER

FLOWING!

God wants us to LIVE IN HIS RIVER!

THIS RIVER IS AMAZING!
THIS RIVER IS EVER-FLOWING!
THIS RIVER COMES FROM GOD AND IT IS A NEVER-ENDING SUPPLY!
Because He HIMSELF is a never-ending supply!

Oh, that we would come to God AND HIS RIVER OF LOVE and believe!
Out of our bellies would flow rivers of this living water,
HIS LIVING WATER!

ALL WOULD BE HEALED!

As long as we are plugged into the source
SUPPLY FLOWS,
HIS SUPPLY!

JESUS is our supply. HE is our source.
Rest in Him!
Stay connected to Him!
Abide in Him and let HIS SUPPLY flow,
His never-ending supply!
HIS RIVER FLOWS!
It is unending!
It is undeniable! It is ever flowing and gets greater the more it flows from the temple!
It grows deeper the further it flows from the temple!

Flow in His river! Flow in His love!
IT WILL GROW DEEPER!
IT CAN ONLY GET DEEPER!
IT CAN ONLY GET WIDER!
IT CAN ONLY FLOW FASTER!

JUST FLOW WITH IT!
JUST FLOW ON TOP OF IT!
JUST RIDE ON TOP OF IT!

It comes from His side!
He was pierced for us
IN LOVE!

BECAUSE OF HIS LOVE,
OUT OF HIS SIDE, FLOWS HIS LOVE!
HIS LOVE FOR US, NOT OUR SIN, PUT HIM ON THE CROSS!
HE ACCOMPLISHED FOR US A WELL OF LIVING WATER…SPRINGING UP FOR US EVERLASTING LIFE, FOREVER!

ABIDE IN THIS RIVER,
THIS FLOWING RIVER,
EVERY DAY,
ALL DAYS,
EVERY WAY,
ALL WAYS!!
AND IT WILL BECOME A NEVER-ENDING FLOW,
DEEPER THAN ANY OCEAN!

AND ALL WHO COME TO IT WILL BE HEALED
AND WILL BE PROVIDED FOR!
IN JESUS IS EVERYTHING!
OUT OF JESUS IS EVERYTHING!
COME TO HIM
AND HE WILL PROVIDE EVERYTHING!
HIS LOVE WILL PROVIDE EVERYTHING,
FOREVER,
IN ALL WAYS,

HIS RIVER,
HIS LOVE!!!

THERE IS A RIVER that makes glad the city of God.

There IS a river.

It is there. It is here.
We just abide in it. We just flow with it. We just ride on top of it.
It makes glad the city of God.
We are HIS CITY.
We are HIS ZION
and HIS RIVER makes us glad!

Come to HIS RIVER. Ride upon it.

RECEIVE HIM!

Receive HIS RIVER and out of your belly will flow RIVERS OF LIVING WATER.

That is His Word.
That His voice.
HIS VOICE sounds like rushing waters.
Those who hear it are raised to life.
Those who hear it come to life from the dead.

His Words are life.
HIS VOICE is life!
HEAR IT!
FLOW WITH IT
and LIVE!

His Words are Spirit and life. His Words are His river.
His love is His river. It is flowing for us.
It is unrelenting. It will not stop. It cannot ebb. We just ride on it.

HIS RIVER!

HIS LOVE

For US!

R-I-V-E-R, Rest In Victory and Eternal Redemption, that is the RIVER!

That is HIS LOVE for us.

That is eternal redemption.
We are living His life out on the earth, NOT OUR OWN!
HIS LIFE FOR US!
We are redeemed. We just rest in it. We just receive it.

We just flow in HIS RIVER.

We just flow in His victory.
We just flow in His eternal redemption.
We just flow in HIS LIFE!
We just rest, forever!

We are redeemed. We are loved!

WE ARE IN HIS RIVER,

FOREVER!

HIS RIVER FLOWS,

FOREVER!

ROARING!

HIS RIVER IS ROARING!
He roars like a lion!

HIS LOVE, HIS VOICE, SURROUNDS US,
PROTECTS US!

He is our king, ROARING to protect us!
His voice surrounds us, loves us, and drives away the enemy!

Submit to God, resist the devil, and he will flee from you.
Speak GOD'S WORDS
and the enemy will flee from you, IN TERROR!
ALL ENEMIES WILL RUN FROM YOU IN TERROR.
HIS VOICE IS LIKE THE SOUND OF MANY RUSHING WATERS!

THIS RIVER IS ROARING!

IT IS SO LOUD THAT MANY CANNOT COMPREHEND IT!
IT IS SO CONSTANT THAT MANY DO NOT PERCEIVE IT!
BUT THIS DOES NOT STOP US!
WE LIVE ON TOP OF IT.
WE LIVE UPON IT!
WE LIVE IN THE MIDDLE OF IT!

We live in the middle of HIS WORDS!

We live in the middle of HIS LOVE!

His roar protects us!

He roars FROM ZION

AND WE LIVE IN THAT ROAR!

HE ROARS
AND ALL ENEMIES FLEE!

ABIDE IN THAT RIVER OF HIS LOVE.
IT IS ROARING!

THE ROAR CARRIES US!
THE RIVER CARRIES US AND CONVEYS ITS POWER!
OTHERS CANNOT COMPREHEND IT!

We are in the middle of the roar, surrounded by it!
IN THE MIDDLE OF THE ROAR WE CANNOT HEAR ANYTHING ELSE.
WE ARE IN THE RIVER OF HIS LOVE!
HIS LOVE, HIS ROARING,
IT DROWNS OUT ALL OTHER VOICES,
FOREVER!

"You're in my river!
Stay in MY river!"

THE VOICE OF ANOTHER WE WILL NOT FOLLOW!
This voice is frightening to the enemy.
This voice is frightening to others.
This voice is frightening to those NOT IN THE RIVER.
But we hear it. We obey and we put fear into our enemies.

HIS VOICE IS A ROAR FROM ZION.

His voice is power.
Others cannot hear the voice.
It has been obscured.
The veil has been left over their faces. To them it just sounds like a dull roar.
They have heard it so long they do not even notice it! That cannot make anything of it.
They cannot understand.

But we are HIS SHEEP. We hear HIS VOICE.
We speak HIS VOICE…and it comes out as a ROAR!
Our enemies flee in terror because we are submitted to God.

We are just flowing in HIS RIVER!

His roar comforts us.
The sound of HIS VOICE
brings us Love, HIS LOVE.

We eagerly hear His voice and the voice of another
WE WILL NOT FOLLOW!
It is His love.
It is His ROAR!
It is HIS RIVER!

His voice is His river.

We just live in it.
We just receive it.
We just follow it.
We just flow with it,

FOREVER!

A male lion roars and scares the prey to the females, then they ambush.
We live under His roar.
It is His voice IN US that scares the enemy.

We win.

We devour everything the enemy is trying to do,
BECAUSE OF GOD'S VOICE,
HIS ROAR, WITHIN US!

We submit to God.
We resist the enemy
and he flees from us.
THE ENEMY FLEES FROM US
IN TERROR,

because we are submitted to the roar that is within us.
We are submitted to the RIVER within us and NOTHING can resist it.
NOTHING can stop it.
It is mighty.
It is HIS ROAR.
Nothing can overcome it.
We overcome everything with it,

WITH HIS ROAR, as HIS CHILDREN, IN HIS RIVER!

It is His river.
It is His world.
We just live in it. We just flow with it.
BECAUSE HE HAS GIVEN IT TO US!

It is His roar.
It is His voice.
We just hear it and act on it. We obey it.

We obey His voice, and nothing can stop it.

IT IS HIS ROAR!

HIS RIVER IS ROARING!

A SUNNY DAY!

We live in a sunny day!

In THE LIGHT OF HIS LOVE every day is a BEAUTIFUL DAY!

The Book of Psalms describes this river, this beautiful, sunny day that we live in:

THERE IS A RIVER whose streams shall make glad the city of God,
The holy place of the tabernacle of the Most High,
God is in midst of her, she shall not be moved;
God shall help her just at the BREAK OF DAWN!
The nations rage, the kingdoms were moved;
HE UTTERS HIS VOICE, THE EARTH MELTED.

The dawn has broken!
REVELATION IS HERE!

He has helped US!
We speak His voice.
We speak His love.
Kingdoms will be moved. The earth will melt!
Because HE IS WITH US!

Every day with God is sunny.

There is no failure in Him.

There is no darkness in Him!

HE IS LIGHT!
IN HIM THERE IS NO DARKNESS AT ALL!

He prospers us in all things.

IN HIM, EVERYTHING we do is successful.

We cannot fail!
It is a sunny day, HIS SUNNY DAY!

What does it mean to be IN HIM, to know your life is not your own?
He has redeemed you.
He has paid for you.
He has bought you for a price!
You are HIS! He owns you!
He is responsible for you.
What a glorious liberty this is!
What a glorious light this is,
to know He is responsible for you,
and the price He paid FOR YOU is such a high one!

Never believe the lie that you are not worth much.
Never believe the lie that there is no value in you.
You are worth what He paid for you.

HE PAID FOR YOU WITH HIS SON, WITH HIS LIFE!

The book of Leviticus commanded us that we shall not eat anything with it's blood, because the LIFE IS IN THE BLOOD!
The life of anything is IN ITS BLOOD.
And that is what has been poured out for you, HIS BLOOD, HIS LIFE!

YOU ARE VALUABLE. YOU ARE IN THE LIGHT OF HIS LOVE!

Oh, that we can rest in the sunshine of that LOVE!

That love that never rests.
That love that never sets!
The love that never goes down.
The love that never decreases…
The love that is always expanding.
The love that never wanes.
The love that is always changing…
AND IS AS BIG AS HIS LIFE, AS BIG AS HE IS!

That love is unrelenting
and it burns up everything not of value in your life,
because YOU ARE THAT VALUABLE!

YOU ARE VALUABLE TO HIM!

Rest in HIS LOVE!
Abide in it! It is always shining.

THAT SUN IS ALWAYS SHINING!

In every way, in all ways, that sun is shining!
The brightness of love endures FOREVER!
We are the light of the world!
Because He is our light! His light shines upon us, because He love us!

Isaiah was given by God the Words to describe this Love:

Arise, shine;
For your light has come!
And the glory of the Lord has risen upon you!
For behold, the darkness shall cover the earth,
And deep darkness the people;
But the Lord will arise over you.
And His glory will be seen upon you.
The Gentiles shall come to your light,
And kings to the brightness of your rising.

Lift up your eyes all around, and see:
They all gather together, they come to you;
Your sons shall come from afar,
And your daughters shall be nursed at your side.

Then you shall see and become radiant,
And your heart shall swell with joy;
Because the abundance of the sea shall be turned to you,
The wealth of the Gentiles shall come to you.
The multitudes of camels shall cover your land,
The dromedaries of Midian and Ephah,
All those from Sheba shall come;
They shall bring gold and incense,
And they shall proclaim the praises of the LORD.
All the flocks of Kedar shall be gathered to you,
The rams of Nabioth shall minister to you;
They shall ascend with acceptance on MY altar,
And I will glorify the house of My glory…

…The sun shall no longer be your light by day,
Nor for brightness shall the moon give light,
And your God your glory.
YOUR SUN SHALL NEVER GO DOWN,
Nor shall your moon withdraw itself;
FOR THE LORD WILL BE YOUR EVERLASTING LIGHT!

He is our light!
He is our EVERLASTING light!
His light never subsides, nor will it!
We stay in the light!
We walk in the light
and the light NEVER goes out.
The darkness cannot comprehend it.

But we walk as children of light.
We bask in it.
We abide in it
FOREVER!

His love!
His light!
On us
FOREVER!

There is no variation or shadow of turning.

He is true.

His love is true.
He will always manifest that TRUE LOVE to his children,

TO US!

Hallelujah!

Every day a sunny day!
Every day a beautiful, sunny day!
IN THE SUNSHINE OF HIS LOVE, FOREVER!

ARISE,

SHINE, FOR YOUR LIGHT HAS COME!

IT IS HERE…
AND WILL NEVER GO AWAY,

THE LIGHT,

THE LIGHT OF HIS LOVE!

EVERY DAY IS A SUNNY DAY
WITH HIM,

IN HIS RIVER!

INNER TUBES

FLOATING

DOWN

Inner tubes,
floating on His LOVE, floating on His Goodness,
His provision!

Our innermost being filled with HIS BREATH!
That is what we rest upon.
That is what conveys us.
HIS BREATH,
which HE PLANNED for us before the foundation of the world,

His breath in our lungs, HIS BREATH IN OUR LIVES!

You have to be resting when riding on an inner tube. Anything but laying down will simply not work for long. Standing up, running, or working will tip you over.

We have to be seated.
We have to be reclining, like John physically reclined on JESUS.
We have to be resting for this to work!

If we spring a leak and let the air out we will sink.
The air has to be sealed inside.
The inner tube has to be rugged and durable.
No rock, no impediment, can puncture it!
HIS BREATH, forever in our lungs.
It buoys us!

NO OUTSIDE INTERFERENCE CAN TAKE THIS BREATH FROM US!
It raises us up and allows us to float on everything in this life.
HIS BREATH,
HIS SPIRIT with OUR REST is unstoppable!

It will float!
IT HAS TO STAY ON TOP, EVEN WHEN PUSHED DOWN!
It will go down the river!

The buoyancy of the air and the current of the river are unstoppable,
WITH OUR REST!
WE REST AND LET THE FLOW HAPPEN!
WE REST AND LET HIS BREATH SUPPORT US!

Even if we fall into the water, the water carries us.
We flow along and just get back on the ride.
He never leaves us nor forsake us!
He does not give US HIS SPIRIT by measure.

He does not give as the world gives.
He does not give…and then take it back.
He does not give…with conditions.
He bequeaths HIS SPIRIT, HIS PEACE to us.
HE WILLS IT TO US!
HE HAS WILLED IT TO US!
HE HAS BEQUEATHED IT TO US,

FOREVER GIVEN IT TO US!

It is given to us by His death and resurrection!
It is His will.
It is His testament.

This is what we rest on.
We rest on HIS SPIRIT, His "ruach", His breath, in our lungs,
His Spirit breathed into us.
Lean into it. Put yourself fully on it.

I love the story of the slave working on his master's plantation. The slave was unflappable. He always seemed at peace. He always was calm. He always had joy. He always had wisdom, even while he was working. Meanwhile the master had no peace, he had no joy, and never could rest. He asked the slave his secret, and the man said "I used to try to stand on the rock that is JESUS, then I would fall. Then I would just sit on the rock that is Jesus, but I still would fall occasionally, and have problems. But when I laid down fully on the rock of Jesus, I could never be shaken, nothing could ever let me down. Nothing could ever effect me! Now I never even raise my head up off of JESUS! I am fully laid out, stretched out flat on HIS LOVE!"

We, like that slave, rest in JESUS!
We spread out totally on Jesus.

We rest on Him like John did, laying in His bosom, on His chest.

HE ENVELOPS US!

He gives His whole life to us.
We just submit to it and lay down on it.
WE IMMERSE OURSELVES…IN HIM!

We just flow with HIS RIVER!

Rest on His air.
Rest on His Spirit.
Let His Spirit surround you!
Let His Spirit carry you!
Let His Spirit support you.
It will NEVER let you down.

You will never fail,
BECAUSE YOU ARE IN HIM!
THERE IS NO FAILURE IN HIM!
THERE IS NO FAILURE IN HIS LOVE!

WE ARE RIDING ON INNER TUBES, FLOATING DOWN…IN HIS RIVER!

EVERYONE

HAS

THEIR OWN

Everyone!

EVERYONE HAS THEIR OWN!
NO ONE CAN IMITATE YOU
NOR SHOULD THEY!

You are unique and their is no one like you
IN ALL THE WORLD!

There is no one like you that has ever been created.
Their is no one like you that will ever be created.

This is a miracle,

the undeniable gift of GOD!

You get to be you and no one else!

Don't believe the lie that God loves us all the same.
It sounds so Biblical
but it is not true!

You cannot measure the love.
It is a special, different love for each one of us!
WE CANNOT MEASURE THE LOVE.

It has been poured out for us.
It has been poured to us and it is immeasurable!

GOD IS LOVE. HE CANNOT BE MEASURED AND HE HAS POURED HIMSELF OUT FOR US!
HE HAS POURED HIMSELF OUT TO US!

HE NEVER CHANGES!
BUT HE CAN NEVER BE DESCRIBED THE SAME WAY TWICE.
HE NEVER DOES THE SAME THING TWICE.
HE NEVER REPEATS HIMSELF.
BUT HE NEVER CHANGES.
HE IS IMMUTABLE

He has a set, defined, divine plan just for you.

It is stored in heaven,
JUST FOR YOU!

IT WAS PLANNED BEFORE THE FOUNDATION OF THE WORLD...
HIS PLAN,
HIS LOVE,
HIS LIFE,
FOR YOU,

and it can never be duplicated!
It can never be replicated!

IT CAN NEVER BE IMITATED.

LIVE YOUR OWN LIFE AND NEVER TRY TO MIMIC OTHERS.

NEVER TRY TO COMPARE YOURSELF TO OTHERS.

YOU ARE YOU!
YOU HAVE YOUR OWN
and no one can ever change that!
No can ever be you!
NO ONE CAN EVER REPLACE YOU!
EVERYONE HAS THEIR OWN
AND YOU ARE HIS OWN!

His uniqueness is upon you.
His set plan is only for you.
No one can take it.
No one can stop it
AND NO ONE CAN IMITATE IT!

IT IS YOUR OWN!!

His new commandment is that we love ONE ANOTHER.
This means we love each person, ONE another, ONE AT A TIME!

We love each person, person to person.
We are all unique, with our own unique situations.
So every one needs their own kind of love, their own kind of LOVE,
at the right time.

THIS IS HIS LOVE;
UNIQUE, TOTAL, UNDENIABLE, AND SET ASIDE FOR EACH OF US.

We are to love one another just as He loves us!

This love is our own!
This inheritance is our own, stored away and undefiled in heaven for us!

He divided His inheritance amongst THEM! BOTH His sons, the prodigal child, who left and squandered, and the older child who stayed home and ignored what he had. One Toiled, one wasted everything, but BOTH DID NOT KNOW WHAT WAS THEIR OWN!

Each had their own! Either of them could decide what to do with it, FREELY!

Not one Word of rebuke did the FATHER give them.

We are free to choose what we do with our inheritance.

We are free to choose what we do with HIS LOVE.

IT IS OUR OWN.
It is ours, to ignore, to waste, or to LIVE IN, FOREVER!

Yours is unlike anybody else's whoever will exist and unlike anybody else's that ever has existed.

Like an inner tube, it surrounds you!
Rest in it!
Abide in it!
IT IS YOUR OWN!

WHAT HE HAS FOR YOU SURROUNDS YOU!
HIS GOODNESS IS ALL AROUND YOU!

Lay down in it, and like the inner tube on the river,
it will take you where you need to go…WITH NO EFFORT!
HE DOES THE WORK!

THE RIVER WILL TAKE YOU ALONG WITH HIS PLAN,
WITH HIS FLOW,

IN HIS RIVER,

IT IS HIS PLAN!
We just take our inheritance and go with it!

IT IS HIS LOVE FOR YOU!
IT IS HIS OWN UNIQUE PLAN FOR YOU!
IT IS HIS OWN UNIQUE LOVE FOR YOU!
IT IS HIS RIVER FOR YOU!

YOU HAVE YOUR OWN!

THE MORE FUN

YOU HAVE...

THE MORE PEOPLE

JOIN IN

FUN!

Fun is a dirty word in so many Christian circles.

But God did not die and live again to make you a Christian.

He made you to be BLESSED!
HE MADE YOU TO BE RIGHTEOUS!
HE MADE YOU TO BE HIS SONS AND DAUGHTERS,
FOREVER SETTLED AND SECURE WITH HIM, IN HIM!

HE MADE YOU TO HAVE FUN!!

HE MADE YOU INTO HIS SONS AND HIS DAUGHTERS.
There is so much excitement, joy, AND FUN that comes with that sonship!
It is indescribable!

This is not a life of boredom.
This is not a life of drudgery.
This is not a life of struggle.
THIS IS A LIFE OF FUN!

This is a flow!
THE MORE FUN YOU HAVE, the more you please Him!
ENJOY HIM!
ENJOY JESUS!
This is a fun life,

AN EASY LIFE!

The way of the transgressor is hard.
But if we abide in Him and do what He says, happiness, easiness, and JOY abounds!

FUN,

THIS IS THE LIFE HE WANTS FOR YOU!

THIS IS THE LIFE HE DIED TO GIVE YOU!

THIS IS THE LIFE HE LIVES TO GIVE YOU!

AS HARD AS IT WAS FOR JESUS, THAT IS AS EASY AS IT IS FOR YOU!

Abide in this easiness.
Dwell in this abundance,
the abundance of His Word,
the abundance of His will for you!

He wants you to have fun.

He wants you to have joy EVERY DAY!

He wants you to be like Him!

He made you like JESUS!

IN HIS PRESENCE IS FULLNESS OF JOY.

Draw near to God and He will draw near to you.

This is the joy.
This is the fullness.
This is the victory.
This is the FUN!

IT IS YOURS, IN HIM!

F-U-N, Fully under newness!

FUN,
THIS IS WHAT WE LIVE IN!
THIS IS WHAT WE EXIST IN.
THIS IS WHAT WE MOVE IN.
THIS IS WHAT WE BREATH!

IN HIM WE MOVE AND HAVE OUR BEING
AND HE IS FUN!

JESUS IS ALWAYS NEW!
HE IS ALWAYS ADVENTURE!
HE IS NEVER BORING!
HE IS ALL OF GOD, FOR YOU, ALL OF THE TIME!

THAT IS THE FUN!
THAT IS THE LIFE
that He won for you by his death and by HIS LIFE!

One of the keys to fun, the keys to JOY, is HIS LOVE.
HE MAKES ALL THINGS NEW!
He is always new.

There is no stagnation in Him.

There is no routine with Him.
He is anything but routine.
He is anything but boring!
He is always exciting!

HE IS ALWAYS FUN!
HE IS FUN IN ALL WAYS!

HE IS ALWAYS TAKING YOU TO NEW THINGS.
This the secret to the fun.
This is the secret to an exciting life
THIS IS THE SECRET TO A LONG LIFE, A FULL LIFE:
HIS NEWNESS
HIS NEW THINGS
HIS LIFE,
IN YOU NOW!

He is always NEW!
He is always NEW!
He is new in ALL WAYS!
He is new every day.

Flow in that newness. Flow in that fun.
That is God. That is who He designed us to be!

HE MAKES ALL THINGS NEW,
ALL THE TIME,
ALWAYS,
ALL WAYS!

Never empty,

never alone,
never routine,
never repeating,
this is the NEWNESS!
This is HIM!

He is living in YOU NOW!
He makes ALL THINGS NEW!

If there is something old in your life, if there is something stagnant, IT IS NOT HIM! GET RID OF IT! IT IS NOT OF HIM!

Flow with the RIVER.

This RIVER cleanses.
This RIVER washes away, continually.
This is the newness,

and where there is newness, THERE IS FUN,
There is excitement,
THERE IS JOY!

That is who He is,
all of His newness,
all of Him,
is FOR YOU NOW
AND FOREVER!

THIS FUN IS FOR YOU TO HAVE!

Hallelujah!

GOD'S MOST FERVENT DESIRE IS FOR US
TO JOIN TO HIM.
God's most fervent desire is for everyone to be
joined to Him,
FOR US TO BE ONE WITH HIM,
FOR US TO BE ONE AS HIM,
FOR US TO BE ONE WITH EACH OTHER AS
HE AND THE FATHER ARE ONE!

He desires that NONE should perish.
HE LOVES for us to LOVE HIM, RECEIVE HIM,

and BE ONE WITH HIM!

He wants His people to join HIM in what He is
doing.
He wants His people to join with Him!
HE WANTS US ALL TO BE ONE, AS JESUS
AND THE FATHER ARE ONE,
TO BE ONE IN US,
TO BE ONE IN HIM!

As you receive others will join.

As we all receive we all become one.
The Holy Spirit is one spirit, not a billion spirits.
When we abide in this ONE SPIRIT we all become one.
When we do what the Holy Spirit says we all become one!
We all become one body.
We are flesh of His flesh.
We are bone of His bone.

We are FOREVER joined to Him and in HIS LOVE!

One of our main jobs as His sheep is to follow the shepherd so others can see Him and follow Him.
It is hard to follow a shepherd that has no sheep following Him.
It is hard to even tell Him apart from the others, from the farmers, if he has no sheep to distinguish Him.

FOLLOW HIM!
DO WHAT HE SAYS,
AND OTHERS WILL TAKE NOTICE,
OTHERS WILL FOLLOW,
and the more that follow the more people want to join in!

That is His desire, for us to be joined with Him,
for ALL to be joined with Him,
to be rooted and grounded in His love.

That is His system; "Apart from me you can do NOTHING".
HE MEANS WHAT HE SAYS: NO THING!
APART FROM HIM WE CAN DO NO THING!
That is the way He designed it, BECAUSE HE LOVES US!

Any branch not connected to the vine is taken aside and burned.

He did it this way because He loves us!
He made it this way because He loves us!
HE WANTS TO BE PART OF EVERY PART OF OUR LIVES, FOREVER!

Abide in that love.
Stay connected to Him and we will be connected with each other.
This will make others want to join in,
His people,
IN LOVE, TOGETHER AS ONE,
IN HIM!

That is what He desires
FOREVER!

Peter said, "Grace and peace be multiplied to you through the knowledge of God and Christ our Lord, as His divine power HAS given to us ALL things that pertain to life and godliness, through the knowledge of HIM, who has called us by glory and virtue."

This grace is the BLESSING of the Lord,
His FAVOR!

This grace is everything He won for us, at the cross and out of the empty tomb.

If death could not hold him, it certainly cannot hold us!

This peace is the SHALOM of God; wholeness, completeness, soundness, nothing missing, nothing broken, all through Him!

His quietness,
His REST,
HIS SHALOM,
IS OURS, FOREVER!

How do we live in this?
How do we live in this grace and peace, this favor and completeness?
Grace and peace are multiplied unto us, by KNOWING HIM.
This is not just head knowledge like you know a friend.
This is as a husband knows a wife.
He actually joins spirits with her, and they become one!

WE JOIN SPIRITS WITH HIM…AND BECOME ONE!

The Bible said Joseph did not KNOW Mary, until after she gave birth to Jesus.
THIS IS WHAT THE FATHER WANTS,
A JOINING WITH HIM!

HE WANTS US MARRIED TO HIM!

Not just knowing about Him
but knowing Him
and living in Him,
living AS HIM,
SHARING OUR LIVES WITH HIM,
SHARING HIS LIFE WITH US,
on earth as it is in heaven!

Know about Him.
Learn who He is.
Learn all He has.
LEARN ALL HE HAS GIVEN TO US!
Forget not all His benefits.

Join your soul to Him.
Receive His spirit.
THEN ALL THESE BENEFITS, HIS GRACE
AND HIS PEACE, WILL FLOW LIKE A RIVER.
THEY WILL MULTIPLY.

THEN OTHERS WILL JOIN IN,
MANY OTHERS…

MULTITUDES!!

We are connected to the vine.
We are the branches!
We can do nothing apart from Him!
We are nothing without Him!
Without Him we are just fit to be cast into the fire and burned.
He has come to burn up this chaff,
this wasted effort, this self-covering.

Your were made FOR HIM, BY HIM and THROUGH HIM,
anything else is just wasted effort.

Stay connected. Stay joined to this vine.
Hear from Him.
DO WHAT HE SAYS!
You will have SUCCESS EVERY TIME.

This is the key to joy!
J-O-Y, JUST ONLY YES!
Just say "YES!" to everything He is telling you.
Just say "YES!" to everything he commands.
You will be successful IN EVERYTHING YOU DO!
YOU WILL NEVER FAIL!

This brings JOY!
This brings JOY overflowing, in buckets!
This is what you were made for,
This connection to the vine,
This obedience to the faith,
THIS JOY!

Hear HIM!
Do what He says,
and LIVE!

Live the life He created for you!
Live the life He created you to live.
Live what He made you to be!

JOINED TO HIM,

rooted and grounded in Love,
rooted and grounded in HIS LOVE!
This will BLESS the entire earth, just as HE BLESSED the entire earth!

This is HIS PLAN for YOU!

To live AS HIM on earth,
ON EARTH AS IT IS IN HEAVEN.

Whatever YOU bind on earth is bound in heaven and whatever you loose on earth is loosed in heaven!

This is what you were made for.
This is what you were created to be!
This is what you are to manifest to the whole earth,
to His whole creation.

His whole creation groans for the manifestation of YOU, as HIS SON AND

DAUGHTER! Be joined to Him! In His presence is the FULLNESS OF JOY, FOREVER!

OTHER WILL SEE…THE FUN, YOU JOINED TO HIM!
AND THEY WILL HAVE TO JOIN IN!
THEY WILL JOIN IN!

THE MORE RELAXED

YOU ARE,

THE FASTER

YOU GO

Do you want to go fast?
Do you want to go far?

THEN STOP!
THEN REST!

When we rest in Him, he goes to work.

LET THE RIVER DO ITS WORK!

When we work and struggle, he rests.
He longs to do things for us.
Unless the Lord builds the house the laborer labors in vain.

This is the way it is done.

He said to Jesus, "Sit at my right hand until I make your enemies your footstool!"
Who makes?
Not us,
Not even Jesus,

THE HEAVENLY FATHER MAKES ALL OUR ENEMIES OUR FOOT STOOL!

We are the body of Jesus.
We are His body.

We are flesh of His flesh
and bone of His bone,
FOREVER CONNECTED TO HIM!

God, one by one, is putting all of our enemies under our feet!

What do we do then?

WE REST!
OUR PART IS TO JUST FLOW WITH WHAT HE IS DOING.

He says to us: "DON'T HELP ME! I HELP YOU!"
He doesn't need our help.
Do what He says when He says it.
He makes EVERY ONE of our enemies our foot stool.

While we rest,
Day by day this victory grows.
Day by day we go faster and farther.
Until the last enemy that is defeated is death itself.

Jesus has accomplished all and finished all.
Now He is resting.

Now He is seated.
He is at the Father's right hand
until THE FATHER makes all His enemies His footstool.
Until HE makes all our enemies OUR footstool.

These past experiences and present enemies are what we rest on.
They are our food.
They are our bread. THESE GIANTS ARE BREAD FOR US!
THEY WILL BE BREAD FOR US!

They teach you and make you stronger.
You ACTUALLY draw strength from your enemies.
You actually draw strength from your failures.
The things coming against you benefit you, when you REST
and let GOD make your enemies YOUR footstool!

THIS IS INEVITABLE!
like a river,
We just rest in it!
We just receive.
We just flow with it, IN HIS LOVE, IN HIS RIVER!

IT ROARS AND IT IS UNSTOPPABLE!

YOU CANNOT FIGHT THE RIVER.
BUT YOU SURE CAN RELAX AND FLOW WITH IT!

Jesus did so many of His miracles on the Sabbath.
Why?
Was he trying to aggravate the Pharisees?
Was he trying to make them mad or show them up?
NO!

This was to say as man rests,
He goes into action.
As we sit,
HE makes our enemies bow down to us.

We must have the courage.
We must have the guts,
TO SIT AND RECEIVE WHAT HE HAS DONE FOR US,
WHAT HE IS DOING FOR US!

We have a divine right to healing because of who we are.

We have a divine right to all He is because of who we are.
We have a divine right to everything He has because of who we are,
Who He has made us!
WE ARE HIS SONS AND DAUGHTERS!

We are FOREVER REDEEMED because of the blood of Jesus.

WE ARE HIS CHILDREN.
THIS MEANS ALL HE HAS IS OURS!
THIS MEANS ALL HE IS IS OURS!

In the Jewish culture the sons and daughters have the rights to all the household.
They are equal with the Father.
They are part of the family, FOREVER.
THE FAMILY IS ONE UNIT, FOREVER!
THE FAMILY IS ONE, FOREVER!

This is how God designed it.
We are not meant to be separated from the Father.
We are not meant to be out on our own.
This is a worldly idea.
This is a lie
and it is not from Him.

We just stay connected to Him and receive all He is, because we are His children.

WE ARE HIS SONS AND DAUGHTERS!

ALL HE HAS IS OURS!

ALL HE IS IS OURS!

WE JUST RELAX AND ENJOY IT!
WE JUST RELAX AND ENJOY HIM!

WE WILL REST AND GO FAR!!
WE WILL REST AND GO FAST,

IN HIS RIVER,
IN HIS LOVE!!!

THE MORE

YOU SPLASH AND KICK,

THE MORE

YOU SPIN AROUND

Splashing seems like it is helping.
Oh, How many things do we do to help God?
What they do is put us into a spin.

HE DOES NOT NEED OUR HELP!
GOD SAYS: "DO NOT HELP ME!
I HELP YOU!"

Lazarus was raised from the grave. His name actually is Eleazar in Hebrew. That means GOD HELPS!

Being confused; wondering what is going on, wondering what is going to happen,
are all symptoms of NOT LETTING HIM DO IT!

"LET ME!…LET YOU!" He says!

He says to us: "Get out of the way!"

Stop fighting.
Stop spinning!

Just rest.
Just BE!

HE HAS ALREADY MADE YOU!

YOU ARE MADE!

You have already been made His righteousness,
MADE TO BE HIS RIGHTEOUSNESS
BEFORE THE FOUNDATION OF THE WORLD!

REST!

BE!

This will stop the confusion!
This will stop the spinning!

Flow with where He is taking you,

ON HIS RIVER,
IN HIS LOVE!

Flow with Him.
FLOW AS HIM!

JUST BE!

God says:
You're in MY river!
You're in MY LOVE!
You're in ME!

Just accept it!
Just go with it!
Receive everything He has won for you!
Receive everything that you already are!
Receive everything He has already made you to BE, IN HIM!

THE MORE YOU SPLASH AND KICK,
THE MORE YOU SPIN AROUND!

WE CAN REST!
WE CAN JUST FLOW WITH HIS RIVER!

...FOR NO REASON!

There is no reason for confusion.
There is no reason for turmoil.

You don't have to splash.
You don't have to kick.

THE RIVER HAS THE POWER.
We just flow with it!
We just ride on top of it!

There is no reason for struggle.
There is no reason…for pain.
He bore our sickness.
He bore our pain.

AS HARD AS IT WAS FOR JESUS, THAT IS AS EASY AS IT IS FOR US!

There is no reason for us to fight this. There is reason for us to receive!
RECEIVE!
WE RECEIVE HIM
AND ALL OF HIS FULLNESS!

Why?
BECAUSE HE LOVES US!
Because He made it ALL AVAILABLE.

HE IS JUST WAITING FOR US TO SAY "YES!"

JUST ONLY YES!
THAT IS THE KEY TO JOY!

We say "YES!"
To who He is!

We say "YES!"
To what He has done!

"YES!" to everything!

"YES!" to every benefit!
He forgives ALL of our sins.
He heals ALL our diseases.
He has redeemed us from the pit
and crowned US with love and compassion.
HIS LOVE,
HIS COMPASSION, we are crowned with them,
FOREVER!

He satisfies OUR DESIRES with good things.
He satisfies OUR MOUTH with good things,
so that our YOUTH IS RENEWED LIKE THE EAGLES!

THERE IS NO REASON NOT TO EXCEPT THIS!
There is no reason not to say "YES!".

He has qualified YOU
IN ALL HIS FULLNESS
TO BE HIM,

TO BE LIKE HIM!

AS HE IS, SO ARE WE IN THIS WORLD!

NOW!

NOW is the time!

NOW is the time to receive.

There is NO REASON to not say "YES!"
There is no reason to struggle.
There is no reason to fight.

THERE IS NO REASON TO KICK.
THERE IS NO REASON TO SPIN AROUND.
THERE IS EVERY REASON TO GO WITH HIS RIVER!

BECAUSE HE LOVES US!

...AND THE MORE

DIFFICULT

IT IS

TO STAY

WITH THE OTHERS!

As we struggle,
as we spin around,
we become separated.
we become separated from our brethren.
HE MADE US ALL TO BE BROTHERS AND SISTERS!
But we can become isolated.

He want us all to be one IN HIM!
He wants us all to one AS HIM!

When we splash,
when we kick,
we spin around,
we lose sight of who we are,
we lose sight of who we are supposed to be with, who we are supposed to be LOVE!

His last prayer was for us to be one
as HE AND THE FATHER ARE ONE.

How?
How do we do this?
WE DON'T SPLASH.
WE DON'T KICK.
WE DON'T SPIN AROUND!

We don't struggle.

We just say "YES!"
and EVERYONE else who says "YES!" will be right there with us!

We don't have to struggle to stay together.
We don't have to struggle to stay one.
We just receive HIM, DO WHAT HE SAYS, BE WHO HE SAYS, and we will be one,

IN HIM,
AS HIM!

Don't struggle.
Don't fight.

JUST BE!

BE ALL HE HAS WON FOR YOU!
BE ALL HE HAS MADE FOR YOU
and we will all be one body!

AS HE IS SO ARE WE, IN THIS WORLD!

Stay together,
IN HIM.

BE ONE,
IN HIM!

Stay together,
AS ONE,
BY FLOWING IN THAT RIVER.
Just go with it. Let the river flow,

AS HE AND THE FATHER ARE ONE,

AS HE AND THE FATHER ARE ONE!

How do we stay together?
How do we have unity, this unity that is so treasured?

UNITY IS NOT GOOD ENOUGH!
HE DESIRES ONENESS,
ONENESS, NOT UNITY,
ONENESS, AS HE AND THE FATHER ARE ONE!

We flow with the RIVER!
We do what He says.
We obey.
We just rest and go with where the RIVER is carrying us!
This will keep us together.
This will keep us as one,
BECAUSE IT IS ALL HIS PLAN!

He has a good plan, and it is for ALL OF US! It is for EACH OF US!

IT IS FOR US TO BE ONE,
AS JESUS AND THE FATHER ARE ONE!
AND ALL OF US ONE WITH THE FATHER,

ONE WITH JESUS!

We don't try to stay together!
We don't kick to bring us close to others.
We don't splash to try to be in a group and we don't paddle to try to keep pace.
These just bring confusion,
we end up spinning around
and losing sight of the others.

These struggles bring frustration, bitterness, and wasted energy!
We just flow.
We just hear.
We just obey.
When we obey, we look up and everyone is with us!
Why?
Because it is HIS PLAN.
BECAUSE IT HIS PLAN
AND HIS GOODNESS!

We just receive
and this keeps us together.
This receiving keeps us one,
BECAUSE JESUS AND THE FATHER ARE ONE!

THE LESS WE SPLASH AND KICK,
THE LESS WE SPIN AROUND…FOR NO REASON!

WE JUST STAY TOGETHER.

THE MORE WE OBEY HIM,
THE MORE WE FLOW WITH HIM,
THE MORE WE FLOW AS HIM,

THE MORE WE ARE ONE,
THE MORE WE STAY WITH EACH OTHER, IN HIS RIVER!

THE MORE DRINKS,

SUNTAN LOTION,

UMBRELLAS,

AND OTHER FUN STUFF

YOU HAVE...

THE MORE PEOPLE

NOTICE

GOD LIKES TO PARTY!

GOD LIKES TO CELEBRATE!

Everything starts with a celebration.
The prodigal son returning, the wedding at Cana, the marriage supper of the lamb,
IT ALL STARTS WITH CELEBRATION!

IT ALL STARTS WITH A PARTY!

If we are not partying, IF WE ARE NOT ENJOYING,
NO ONE will notice.
NO ONE WILL COME!

We need to stay together.
We need to stay as one.
We will be one in HIM
AND WE WILL CELEBRATE!

The more we receive,
the more people notice and want to join in!

The more we flow in HIS BLESSING, the more others will notice!
It is HIS LOVE,
we should praise Him for it!

It is His party.
HE is throwing it! IT IS SET UP AND FULLY SUPPLIED!
We should accept the invitation and come in!
This will bring others!
This will show them HIS LOVE and HOW WONDERFUL IT IS
TO BE LOVED BY HIM!

They will not see it if we do not celebrate, If we do not accept it!

Receive Him.
THERE WILL BE CELEBRATION,
EVERY TIME!

You don't need to force yourself to worship or praise.
When you know Him and understand Him you will shout for joy.
We will be victorious EVERY TIME in the name of our God.
WE CANNOT LOSE!
WE WIN EVERY TIME!
WE CELEBRATE EVERY TIME!
WE PARTY EVERY TIME!

It is like a football team that scores every time they touch the ball. Every play, a run, a pass, whatever they do, they score. Whatever play they run, they score. They always get a touchdown. The celebration moves from the end zone, after the score, to the huddle, before the play! The celebration moves all over the field. Even when they are running the play and doing the plan they are celebrating. Even when they are planning and deciding their next move they are already celebrating, BECAUSE THEY GET THE VICTORY EVERY TIME!

Know Him!
Know His love, and how much He protects us.
This will shift you from waiting TO
CELEBRATING!

CELEBRATE,
NOW,
EVERYWHERE,
ALWAYS!

CELEBRATE
HIM!
Worship Him!
Give Him worth (That is what worship means)

BECAUSE HE GIVES US THE VICTORY
EVERY TIME!

We are more than conquerors through Him.

GOD wants us to have abundance.
He wants us to receive
ALL OF HIM!

When we receive and flow in His BLESSING
people will have to notice.

THEY WILL HAVE TO JOIN IN!

No one wants to join into sinking inner tubes
with leaks.
No one wants to join into splashing, spinning
around, and struggling.

People want to join into ABUNDANCE,
FULLNESS, and JOY!

They will see our praise.

THEY WILL SEE OUR PARTYING.
THEY WILL SEE OUR CELEBRATING.
THEY WILL COME
AND JOIN IN!

THEY WILL JOIN HIS RIVER, HIS LOVE!

Do you want people to notice?
Do you want people to join in?
Do you want them to FOLLOW JESUS?
Do you want the whole world to JOIN HIM?

Then BE BLESSED!

Show them the BLESSING to such a degree and they will HAVE TO JOIN IN!

They will HAVE TO ASK you:
"What is going on?
"How do you do this?"
"Where did you get all this?"
Then you can tell them!

They will have to join in!
They will have to JOIN HIM!

THAT IS WHAT HE WANTS!

It was hard for the Pharisees and religious leaders to argue with the healing power of Peter and John when the lame man they just healed is dancing and shouting behind them!

DANCE, SHOUT, JUMP, RECEIVE all He has done for YOU
and no one will be able to argue!
THEIR ARGUMENTS WILL BE FOOLISH!
They will have to join in!

RECEIVE HIS BLESSING TO SUCH A DEGREE THAT THEY WILL HAVE TO NOTICE!

They will HAVE TO join in!
They will throw their old idols to the rocks, the bats, and the caves.
Then they will receive God!
Who wants pale imitations and idols when they can receive the living God,
and BE ALL THAT HE IS?

AS HE IS, SO ARE WE IN THIS WORLD!

Who can say no to this when they get the revelation, when they see it in real life, when it has manifested right in front of them?

RECEIVE,
RECEIVE,
RECEIVE,
and people WILL notice.

IT IS AS BIG AS YOU WANT IT TO BE.

IF HE FREELY GAVE US JESUS, HOW CAN HE NOT FREELY GIVE US ALL THINGS?

When it gets big.
When it gets large and we are in our large place,
OTHERS WILL TAKE NOTICE.
They will have to take notice!

You cannot ignore the bigness of the BLESSING!
You cannot resist the FULLNESS of the BLESSING when it is the FULLNESS OF GOD!

HIMSELF,
He HIMSELF will be our reward!
HE IS OUR REWARD!

When we receive,
others will have to notice,
others will have to join in!

HE IS THAT GOOD!
HE IS THAT ENORMOUS!
HE IS THAT LOVING!

RECEIVE HIM
to bring others into the kingdom, to bring others to HIM!
THIS BRINGS OTHERS INTO HIS LOVE.
THAT IS WHAT HE WANTS!

HE WILL LOOK AT YOU AND SAY "WELL DONE, MY GOOD AND FAITHFUL SERVANT!" when you put HIS BLESSING to work and this brings HIS CHILDREN into HIS KINGDOM!

They will accept it!
They will accept Him WHEN THEY SEE HIS GOODNESS.

IT IS THE GOODNESS OF GOD THAT BRINGS US TO REPENTANCE!!!

He wants everyone in the world to notice!
He wants everyone He has created to notice.
When you receive from Him they will have to notice!

They will have to join in!

THEY WILL HAVE TO FLOW WITH HIS RIVER!

THE MORE YOU

STAY TOGETHER,

THE MORE PEOPLE

NOTICE...

AND WANT TO

JOIN IN

We are meant to be ONE,
as He and the Father are ONE.

JESUS prayed this right before the cross.
Right before the passion, everything He went through,
He prayed that we may know Him,
so we can all be one.
Others would then see us and know we have the Holy Spirit.
They would know we have Him.

This oneness comes from one thing.
It comes from flowing with the river.
When He tells you to do something, do it.
When He tells you to rest, do it.
When He tells you to not say something, don't say it.
When He tells you to not do something, don't do it!
HE IS YOUR LORD!

When this obedience comes, this abiding in the river, we will all be together.
We will all be the body of Christ,
because He is the head
and we listen to Him.

We follow Him!

He showed me a vision of a huge, beautiful, cold, mountain. It was vast and tall. There were numerous multitudes standing around the base. They were just black outlines, silhouettes scattered throughout the trees. They couldn't see each other. They weren't even looking at each other. They seemed focused on their own problems. Then He gave me this revelation. He said "THE PEAK OF THE MOUNTAIN IS A POINT!" What this means is when we leave the low base area and go up to where He calls us, to where He has already placed us, WE ALL HAVE TO BE TOGETHER. We will all be face to face! We will all be in the clear.

THE PEAK OF THE MOUNTAIN IS A POINT!
We will all be together!

Stay at the top of the mountain.

Stay living the high life not the low life.

Listen to Him.
DO WHAT HE SAYS!
INCLINE YOUR EAR!

We will all be together.

Live in His river
and we will all be together, FOREVER!
This will happen automatically.
We will all be one body.

HIS BODY.

We will all be moving together like legs
working together, walking,
like arms coming together to hug,
like hands and arms swinging together to pick
someone up.

We will all be in such oneness that others will
HAVE TO NOTICE!

This oneness is what He wants!
This oneness is what He prayed for so long
ago.
It is His desire,

FOR US TO BE ONE,
AS HE AND THE FATHER ARE ONE!

THE MORE WE STAY TOGETHER,

THE MORE PEOPLE NOTICE!

People want to bring others into the Kingdom.
Believers want to spread their joy to others.
But so often it seems difficult.
So often it seems like a dead work.

Many people hear, receive for awhile, and then go back to what they were.

The solution?

The solution is HIM,
abiding in HIM!
We are to receive Him and live His life out on this planet.

WE DO WHAT HE SAYS!
We will all be together.
We will all be one.

Others will have to notice.
They will see our LOVE.
They will see how we are BLESSED.

They will see our flow.
THEY WILL SEE OUR RIVER!
They will want to join in.

They will have to join in.

THIS IS WHAT THE FATHER WANTS, FOR ALL TO JOIN IN,
FOR ALL TO JOIN TO HIM!

You won't even have to convince them.
You won't even have to ask them!
They will just come in.

We are not selling insurance.
We are not selling vacuum cleaners.
This is not a pyramid scheme.

THIS IS HIM!

THIS IS JESUS!

THIS IS GOD!

When we manifest Him,
when we are in ONENESS
together with Him,
they will come.
They will have to come!

He wants all His children to freely receive.

He wants them all to voluntarily come in their own free will.
He wants them to come, because they love Him!

HE WANTS US ALL IN HIS RIVER, BECAUSE HE LOVES US!

THE MORE YOU TALK AND PRAISE WITH EACH OTHER, THE MORE PEOPLE NOTICE!

Believers say they want to be in fellowship.
They say they want to be together.
They say they want to praise.
But it doesn't seem to happen much,
so many divisions,
so many split apart,
so much separateness!

What is the answer?
Receive what He has done for you!
Receive HIS PLAN!
Receive HIM!

When we all experience the fullness,
We will praise!
We will talk with each other.
We will fellowship.

That is what He does.
He draws people to Him.
When He manifests HIMSELF TO US, others will come!

They will have to come!
They will have to notice.
They will want to join in.

What is our job?
Our job is JUST TO FLOW WITH HIM, ON HIS RIVER,
JUST TO RECEIVE!
OUR JOB IS JUST TO RECEIVE, HIM!

When we do receive,
we will not have any choice but to share Him.
We will talk with each other.
We will praise with each other.

HE IS THAT AWESOME!
HE IS THAT GOOD!

Study His benefits. In the Bible there are more than seventy one hundred promises JESUS won for us, and counting!

Study Him!

It will bring praise.
It will bring fellowship.
It will bring togetherness.

He does that.

Draw near to Him

and other believers will be right there with you.

Do what He says and you will be in fellowship.

He loves it when His people are together IN FELLOWSHIP WITH HIM,
ONE WITH HIM!

The more we talk and praise, the more people notice,
THE MORE PEOPLE GET IN THE RIVER!

FLOW

IN MY

RIVER!

The FLOW,

It is His flow,

flowing out of us like rivers of living water.

His Words are SPIRIT
and they are LIFE!

It is HIS LIFE
and it FLOWS!

It flows like a river.
It gets deeper and deeper!
The further we go with Him, the deeper it gets.
Eventually people cannot get across it!

EVERYONE WILL BE AFFECTED BY YOU,
BECAUSE OF HIS LOVE!

HIS RIVER,
HIS LIFE, FLOWING OUT OF YOU!

Freely love!
Only worship!
The FLOW
that is His love!

HIS LOVE DOES NOT DEMAND.
It does not come with a price.
We do not purchase it. It is free.

Like a river, HIS LOVE is free.
Like a river, it is wild, untamable, and cannot be stopped.
HIS LOVE FOR US will not stop until it reaches the sea,
the sea of HIS GRACE,
the sea of HIS LOVE!

HIS LOVE is ever flowing and ever getting stronger.

FLOW WITH IT!
FLOW WITH HIS RIVER!

It is only getting stronger!
It is only getting deeper!

Every one of our enemies is being made our foot stool, NOW and forever,
Because of THIS LOVE HE HAS FOR US.

It is because of HIS RIVER
LIVING IN US AND FLOWING OUT OF US!

YOU ARE

IN

MY

RIVER!

We ARE in the river.

WE ARE IN HIS RIVER.

Nothing can take that away from us.

It is blood bought. IT WAS BOUGHT WITH HIS LIFE!

It is certain. We are just to receive it. We are just to act like it.

NO SPLASHING! NO KICKING!
No spinning around!
What a waste! What a denial of what He has done for us!
What denial of all He has won for us!

RECEIVE, RECEIVE, RECEIVE,
that you are in HIS RIVER.

It is HIS PLAN!
It is a good one.

IT IS BIG!

It is awesome.
It is amazing.

IT IS AS BIG AS GOD!

WE JUST SAY "YES!"
BECAUSE WE ARE ALREADY IN IT!

WE ARE ALREADY IN HIS RIVER BECAUSE
OF WHAT JESUS DID FOR US!
WE ARE ALREADY IN HIS PLAN
BECAUSE OF WHO JESUS IS FOR US!

R-I-V-E-R: The river is remaining in victory and eternal redemption.
THE VICTORY IS NOW!
THE REDEMPTION IS ETERNAL!
THE REDEMPTION IS FOREVER!

That is JESUS!

That is what HE won for us!

Victory NOW!

VICTORY TODAY
AND IT IS ETERNAL!
This redemption is eternal and cannot be stopped.

We are in HIS LIFE and we just flow with it, as a RIVER!

YOU ARE IN THE RIVER OF HIS LOVE!

ENJOY

MY

LOVE!

Love is laying down your life for your friends.
Love is not a feeling.

Feelings come out of love,
but love is not a feeling.

Love is not that mushy feeling you get when
you like someone, when you are interested.

LOVE IS ACTUALLY DOING SOMETHING!
LOVE IS AN ACT!
LOVE IS ACTIVE!
LOVE IS AN ACTION!
LOVE IS LAYING DOWN YOUR LIFE FOR
YOUR FRIENDS.

When we receive His love,
When we receive His life,
ENJOYMENT is on the other side.

Knowing that someone so powerful and
someone so awesome has laid down HIS LIFE
for you is an amazing revelation.
It will bring peace
and we should ENJOY it!

WE SHOULD ENJOY HIM!

WE SHOULD ENJOY…
WHAT HE HAS DONE FOR US,
WHAT HE HAS CREATED FOR US,
WHAT HE HAS ACCOMPLISHED FOR US!

We can enjoy every moment of this love.
We enjoy every moment…all the time!
We can experience every bit of HIS LOVE!
We have been created for this, TO RECEIVE HIM, TO RECEIVE HIS LOVE!

This love is His life laid down for us.
It is His tangible life laid down for us.

God told me "What good does it do to wish someone well, to say 'Depart be warm, and filled!' If you do nothing for the body?"
He said: "THIS APPLIES TO ME AS WELL!"
God cannot say He loves you, if He does not tangibly do things for you,
if He does not lay His life down for you!

HE BLESSES,
AND BLESSES,
AND BLESSES
BECAUSE OF HIS LIFE,
BECAUSE OF HIS LOVE,

BECAUSE OF JESUS LAYING DOWN HIS LIFE!

We are to just enjoy it!
We are to just enjoy this love!
We are to enjoy HIS LOVE!

IT HAS BEEN SEALED IN HEAVEN FOR US,

BY HIS BLOOD,

FOREVER!

We are to enjoy HIM!

That is what HE WANTS:

ALL OF US IN HIS RIVER, IN HIS LOVE!

ENJOY

ME!

He is personal.
He is a close God.
He is a VERY PRESENT HELP in times of trouble.

He is not just an idea.
He is not just a concept
and HE IS CLOSER THAN YOU THINK.

HE SAYS "WE CAN'T GET ANY CLOSER!"

Jesus has forever destroyed separation from God.
The veil has been torn FROM TOP TO BOTTOM!

Nothing can ever separate us again.

Nothing can ever separate us from His love.

He wants us to enjoy HIM
and to not be self-conscious about it.

That is why we have to be clean.
That is why we have to be righteous.
That is why He had to make us whole, so we can come boldly to His presence and enjoy HIM!

WE NOW CAN COME BOLDLY to His throne of grace.
JESUS MADE US THAT WAY,
THE RIGHTEOUSNESS OF GOD!

He is a living,
breathing,
SPIRIT.

He can be related to, as a person.
He is a person.

Enjoy Him!
Talk to Him!
Hear from Him!

LET HIM GUIDE YOU!

I PROMISE YOU, YOU WILL ENJOY IT!
YOU WILL ENJOY HIM!!!
He wants to spend every moment with you.
HE LOVES YOU THAT MUCH!

He wants to join HIS LIFE TO YOURS.

HE WANTS YOU TO LIVE AS ONE.

ONE IN HIM
AND ONE IN US!
As Him, for Him, and by Him,
that is how he wants us to live!

He loves us so much that He gave us HIS ONLY BEGOTTEN SON.
Can you imagine how much joy comes on the other side of that?

You should!

Try to imagine it.
Try to perceive this BLESSING,
This LOVE that comes with Him giving us HIS ONLY SON!

It is bigger than the universe!
It is bigger than everything HE created!

THIS BLESSING is AS BIG AS HIM!
We are to enjoy every bit,
ALL OF IT!
EVERY PART OF HIM LAID DOWN FOR US, IS FOR US!

It is because HE LOVES US!

Enjoy this love!

ENJOY HIM!

ENJOY HOW AWESOME THIS LOVE IS,
WHAT IT HAS BECOME!

He guides us and tells us ALL THINGS.
HE HOLDS NOTHING BACK
HE IS HOLDING NOTHING BACK!
IT IS AS BIG AS WE WANT IT TO BE,

RIGHT NOW!

Don't deny this truth,
That HE LOVES YOU.

He has given all of Himself to you.
He has given all of Himself for you…
and WE ARE TO ENJOY IT!
WE ARE TO ENJOY HIM,
BECAUSE HE LOVES US,
AND HE HAS MADE HIMSELF AVAILABLE!

ENJOY HIM!
That is what HE wants.

He is personal.

He wants us to know everything about Him.
He is close.

He is holding nothing back from us, especially HIMSELF.

I was laying at JESUS' feet, looking at Him, in the spirit, I started looking at His feet. I started looking at His toes. They were beautiful! They are beautiful! HE is all together lovely. Everything about Him is beautiful, interesting and amazing!

ASK HIM ABOUT HIM!
HE WILL TELL YOU!

HE WILL SHOW YOU!
HE WILL MANIFEST HIMSELF TO YOU!
HE HAS MANY SIDES
AND THEY ARE ALL BEAUTIFUL!

THEY ARE ALL LOVELY!
THEY ARE ALL FOR US TO ENJOY!

WE ARE TO ENJOY HIM!

WE ARE TO ENJOY THE RIVER…
OF HIS LOVE!

ENJOY

MY

LIFE!

Enjoy means "To feel or perceive with pleasure; to take pleasure or satisfaction in the experience of."

It also means "to possess with satisfaction."

He wants you to enjoy HIS LIFE!
He wants you to ENJOY HIM!
HE WANTS YOU TO POSSESS HIM!
HE WANTS YOU TO POSSESS ALL OF HIS PROMISES!

POSSESS THEM WITH SATISFACTION!
ENJOY HIM!

No part of this road is rocky.
No part of this RIVER is dangerous.

It is all pleasure! It is all good!
It is all satisfaction!

We experience Him
and HE ALWAYS satisfies us.

IF WE DELIGHT OURSELVES IN HIM, HE GIVES US THE DESIRES OF OUR HEART.

WE LACK NO GOOD THING.

AT HIS RIGHT HAND ARE PLEASURES FOREVER MORE!

He ALWAYS leads us to green pastures.
He ALWAYS leads us to lay down beside still waters.

This is a good river.

This is a flowing river.

This is a great river, a river of HIS LOVE,
poured out for us.
It is pouring out for us.
It is pouring out of us,
if we can receive it,

IF WE CAN PERCEIVE IT!

BEHOLD! I AM DOING A NEW THING! SHALL YOU NOT PERCEIVE IT?

It is pouring out of us, if we can see it.

BEHOLD, I am doing a NEW thing!
Can you not perceive it?

I am making roads in the wilderness and
RIVERS in the dessert!
This is HIS abundance.
This is His fullness!

It never runs dry, not even in the dessert.
It makes everything green, EVERGREEN.

This is pleasure.
This is satisfaction.

The goodness of God, His enjoyment, and His satisfaction,
are OURS,

IF WE JUST LIE BACK AND FLOW WITH THEM,
IF WE JUST RECEIVE,
IF WE JUST SAY "YES!".

The reason He set up this whole thing,
this whole planet,
this whole universe,
all of creation,

IS SO WE CAN ENJOY HIM,
IS SO WE CAN RECEIVE FROM HIM,
IS SO WE CAN RECEIVE HIM!

We are GIFT RECEIVERS, THAT IS ALL WE ARE,
THAT IS ALL HE MEANT FOR US TO BE!

It has all been done so we can enjoy HIS LIFE!
It is so HE can enjoy US!

He loves to fellowship with us.
He loves to have us flow in HIS RIVER.

Rest, receive, and enjoy HIM!

Enjoy HIS LIFE!

MY!

WE ARE HIS!
HE OWNS US!.

He owns you.

For some that is hard to say.
That is hard to hear for many people.

BUT YOU ARE OWNED!

HE BOUGHT YOU WITH A PRICE.
You are His property.
YOUR LIFE IS NO LONGER YOUR OWN!

YOU ARE HIS
AND HE LIVES IN YOU,
NOW, TODAY!

What does this mean?
We hear.
We obey.
We do what He says.
We obey that voice inside us.
We obey that Holy Spirit inside us.

That is His life.
That is His wisdom.

We were never made to be apart from Him.
He designed us to need Him.
He designed us to be in perfect fellowship with Him, married to Him.

WE ARE HIS BRIDE!

His life is ours
and our life is His.

MY LIFE!
Know what this means.

This may sound bad.
You may ask "What about my plan?"

Well, His plan is THE BEST for you.
His plan is what you want, whether you know it or not!

The BEST PLAN FOR YOU is no different from His, no different from what He wants!
He wants you living as Him,
through Him and for Him,
IN HIS PLAN.

This is exactly what you want.

It is exceedingly abundantly above all you could ask or think,
but IT IS WHAT YOU WANT!

IT IS EVERYTHING YOU WANT!

SUBMIT TO IT!
SUBMIT TO HIS PLAN FOR YOU!

Submit to the fact you are His property.
Submit to the fact your life is no longer your own.

Joy is on the other side.

THAT IS THE RIVER.
We just flow with it.

That is who we ARE!

JUST BE!

JUST BE HIS!

Always and ALL WAYS,
WE ARE HIS!!!

He guides our steps and leads us to green pastures.
HIS LIFE, HIS LOVE, is a roaring, beautiful, RIVER!

It is a river of ABUNDANCE
and it is flowing for us.

It will flow out of us, It will flow around us, and take us places we never could imagine
if we submit to it.

If we say "YES!"

....LIFE!!!

HIS LIFE, in US,

that is what He came to win us.

He did not fail.
We do not fail.

We flow in His river.

His river is His life,
poured out for us!

Leviticus says you cannot eat anything with
its' own blood, because the blood is the life!

HIS BLOOD IS HIS LIFE
AND IT WAS POURED OUT FOR US!
IT WAS POURED OUT FOR YOU!

The blood is the core of every living being.
It can be frightening to see your own blood.
The blood is your inner core, who you are.
Without your blood, there is no life.

HE POURED OUT HIS INNER CORE, WHO HE
WAS, FOR US!
HE POURED OUT HIS LIFE FOR US!

AND NOW
HE LIVES FOR US!

We have conquered the grave and live settled and secure IN HIM!
He came so that WE may have life and have it more abundantly, to the full, until it overflows!

RECEIVE IT!
FLOW WITH IT!
THAT IS WHAT HE WANTS!

US…TO LIVE IN HIS RIVER!

US….LIVING IN HIS RIVER,

FOREVER,
WITH HIM, FOREVER,

IN HIS RIVER!

Inner tubes floating down,

THE RIVER OF GOD,

THE RIVER OF GOD'S LOVE,

Won BY JESUS for YOU!

www.ingramcontent.com/pod-product-compliance
Lightning Source LLC
Chambersburg PA
CBHW051405290426
44108CB00015B/2161